D1714391

**Babylonian slingers from the Nimrud reliefs, c. 800 BC, in
the British Museum.**

THE SLING

FOR SPORT & SURVIVAL

Cliff Savage

Loompanics Unlimited
Port Townsend, Washington

THE SLING
© 1984 by Loompanics Unlimited

Published by:
Loompanics Unlimited
PO Box 1197
Port Townsend, WA 98368
Loompanics Unlimited is a division of Loompanics Enterprises, Inc.

Cover and illustrations by Kevin Martin

ISBN 0-915179-19-9
Library of Congress Card Catalog 84-81630

Contents

1

Introduction

In early prehistoric times, there was not much to distinguish man from his fellow higher primates. All walked on their hind legs, all found food by gathering and hunting, all species even used stones and sticks to aid their efforts. One of the first abilities that distinguished man from other developed animals was the use of tools other than sticks and stones. The sling was one of the first of these tools.

The first slings were most likely made of a strip of animal hide slightly wider in the middle than at the ends. Prehistoric man used this simple device to hurl stones further than they could be thrown by hand. Slowly it was discovered that this tool had a multitude of uses. It could of course be used to fend off an attacking animal (or human). It could be used to hunt for animals from a safer distance. It could be used to knock fruit out of high trees. It wasn't long before the sling became an indispensable and universally used tool.

Through the ages, the sling has continued to be used while other weapons have come and gone. From prehistoric times until the middle ages, the sling was an essential weapon in any war. In hunting and agriculture it remained popular. With the advent of gunpowder, the sling began to diminish in use. New weapons were discovered to hurl stones (or bullets) much faster and farther than a man could accomplish with the sling. But the sling has never died out.

The sling may not be a popular weapon today, but it is certainly still a valuable one. For example, the sling is an ideal weapon for urban warfare and street fighting. In Northern Ireland and the Philippines, the sling often sees use in skirmishes between the police and rebels. As we shall see, the sling is hardly a weapon whose time has passed. It simplicity and versatility are properties that make for endurance. The times we are living in may lead to a rebirth of the sling such as hasn't been seen for a thousand years.

In this book, we will examine the sling and its uses thoroughly. We will study its historical uses and see why the sling was such an important weapon. We will take a look at the sling as a weapon and see what advantages it holds over other weapons. We will illustrate the variety of ways the sling can be used. We will demonstrate the methods for constructing slings from the simple to the elaborate. We will look at the ammunition used, and how it can be improved. Lastly, we will tell you how the sling can be applied in modern situations. You will see that the potential for the sling is barely limited, and that its practicality and adaptability for modern use is astounding.

History of The Sling

The exact origin of the sling is difficult to determine, because the actual device decomposed, and because the ammunition, being mere stones, is not distinctive to archaeologists. The sling was man's first missile weapon. It is likely that the sling was the first long-distance weapon. It certainly predated the bow, and is believed to go back in history at least 10,000 years.

What we call a sling probably developed from a simpler weapon: a stone attached to a length of vine or leather or animal sinew. This early primitive device was swung then thrown at the target from a safe distance. The problem with this weapon was that it had to be retrieved after use, and that it simply was not very effective. This rope-and-stone is believed to be the immediate predecessor of two popular weapons that are still in use today: the sling, and the bola.

The relationship between the primitive weapon described above and the sling and bola is illustrated below. The bola consists of three ropes attached together at one end, and attached to three stones or metal balls at the other ends of the ropes. When thrown with skill, it injures the prey either by hitting it, or tangling around its legs and tripping it up. The sling separates the rope and stone, so that the rope can be reused, while the stone need not be retrieved. Both weapons were large improvements in design over the primitive rope-and-stone. They are faster, more accurate, and hit with deadly force.

A rock tied to a piece of rope or vine (top) led to the creation of the bola (right) and the sling (left).

One of the amazing facts about the history of the sling is that traces of its use can be found in nearly every region of the world. Historical records show that the sling was used in Asia, Africa, North and South America, the Middle East, and particularly in Europe. There are also records of the sling's use on many Pacific Islands. Archeologists have found piles of literally thousands of rounded stones that could have been stored for no other reason.

The Bible has several references to the sling, the most famous of which is the story of David and Goliath. In the First Book of Samuel, the Bible says that "David put his hand in his bag, and took thence a stone, and slang it, and smote the Philistine in his forehead, that the stone sunk into his forehead; and he fell upon his face to the earth." This brief encounter illustrates exactly how useful the sling was in early history.

David was a small guy, and Goliath a giant by historical standards. In hand-to-hand combat, David didn't stand a chance. With the sling, however, he could keep his distance. David had been a shepherd before joining the ranks of Saul's army. As a shepherd, he was very familiar with the use of the sling, since it was used to keep the flock from straying too far, and to ward off any dangerous predators.

Saul tried to load David up with armor and weapons, but the young warrior would have none of it. His big advantage was his mobility. Goliath was covered with armor, a shield, a helmet, and leg gear. As such, Goliath could not easily move to chase David. The distance David was able to keep from the giant gave him the operating room he needed.

David was a very good shot. When he hit Goliath in the forehead, he struck the only unprotected part of the giant's body. Such accuracy is probably not an exaggeration. Had David missed, he still had four other stones to hurl against his enemy. He was confident enough of his shot to feel certain that he would fell the giant in five shots.

There are other references to slingers in the Bible, too. The Book of Judges proclaims the ability of the left-handed slingers of Benjamin, who inflicted heavy casualties against the Israelites: "Every one could sling stones at a hair breadth, and not miss." Other biblical accounts of slingers are made in the Second Book of Chronicles and the Second Book of Kings.

There is reference made to the sling in Homer's Iliad, but only briefly in passing. One reason that there are not more accounts of slinging in ancient texts is that it was not considered a noble form of combat as hand-to-hand combat was. But that does not mean slinging was not an important military tool.

Peltists, which included slingers, archers, and javelin throwers, were usually the initial combat force in battle during classical Greek times. Their blows exposed weak points in the enemy formation which the armored infantry then attacked. If the battle was going the wrong way, the peltists provided enough time for retreat, since armored warriors were burdened by their heavy coats. Indeed, the historian Manfred Korfmann in his article "The Sling as a Weapon," (see *Bibliography*) states that "Any army that entered battle without peltists was as good as defeated."

Other notable historical accounts of the sling being used as a military weapon can be found. In 401 B.C., the Greeks attempted to overthrow the King of Persia. A force of 10,000 Athenians led by Xenophon were nearly wiped out by the Persians. Xenophon noted that his slingers "carried farther with their missiles than the Persians, farther even that the Persian bowman." (Korfmann, *The Sling as a Weapon*.)

A Greek peltist is shown above with his sling. Hurlers
played an important role in the armies of ancient Greece.

The most famous slingers of antiquity were the natives of the Balearic Islands off the coast of Spain. The Balearic slingers served as lightly-armored peltists in many of the wars during classical times. They would carry three lengths of sling with them: a short one for short-range, a long one for distance shots, and a medium one for somewhere between. Slinging was of much importance to the Balearians that their mothers would not allow them to eat until they hit their marks in practice. One form of training involved slinging a stone through a narrow hoop from a substantial distance.

The art of slinging was refined considerably as it progressed. Its importance is attested to by ancients finds of thousands of bullets specially manufactured for the sling. Some of these were made from clay, others from lead. The shape was refined from spherical at first, to biconical (pointed at both ends) and finally to an ovoid shape like a small egg.

These manufactured bullets had many advantages over stones. Their shape and weight nearly doubled the potential range of a slinger. They could be manufactured at the battle site without having to send soldiers out to carry a heavy load of stones back to camp. Most importantly, their uniformity meant that the slinger would not have to adjust his throw with each new stone. The slingers were able to perfect their throws much easier with this sophisticated ammunition.

The average weight of the manufactured sling bullets was approximately one ounce. Often times the molds used to make them were inscribed with messages that then appeared on the missiles. Some of these messages were the names of famous slingers, or the names of the commanders of the troops or their city of origin. Some messages were as simple and humorous as "Take That!" or "Ouch!" The inscriptions on these bullets have provided important historical information as to the commanders of ancient battles.

The popularity of the sling did not decline with the rising influence of the bow. This is probably because slingers could still hurl stones further than a bowman could send his arrow. In ancient Greece and Rome, the two weapons were used side by side. Korfmann, however, suggests that the bow and sling were mutually exclusive in many areas of the world ("*The Sling as a Weapon*"). That is, most people preferred to use one to the exclusion of the other. On certain Pacific Islands, where the sling was an extremely popular weapon, the introduction of the bow never reduced the use of the sling.

The sling continued to be a popular and important weapon throughout the middle ages. It was developed to a precise instrument, and led to the construction of new weapons. The staff sling, which is nothing but a sling attached to the end of a stick, was used to hurl large ammunition with greater force during the sieges of many a fortress. The sling was also inspired development of the catapult and extremely large catapults called trebuchets and mangonels. These larger devices were erected during a siege, and were sometimes used to sling diseased animals (even horses) into the enemy fortress (see *Weird and Wonderful Weaponry* in the *Bibliography*).

The popularity of the sling diminished with the advent of gunpowder, but still found limited use. Of particular importance was the use of the sling to hurl grenades at enemies or at their forts. The use of slings gradually declined, however, as guns came to be the major device for hurling pellets. By the eighteenth century, use of the sling as a weapon was confined to primitive areas of the world where guns had not yet been introduced.

Changing technology may well bring the sling back as a popular weapon. The growth of urban centers in the twentieth century and the restrictions placed on the ownership of weapons are giving a new twist to the sling. Its peculiar properties make it a valuable weapon of self-defense in today's industrial cities. As we shall see later, the sling still has many uses that could keep it in circulation for centuries to come.

3

The Sling as a Weapon

Basic Description

The most general form of the sling is a cord of leather or sinew with a pocket in the center. Often the cord is in two pieces, tied or sewn to each side of the pocket. The pocket is called "socket," and is usually made of leather or some other durable material. One side of the cord is called a "retention cord," and has a loop tied in the end called the "retention shank." The retention shank slips over a finger of the throwing hand to hold the sling in place when hurling. The other side is called a "release cord." A knot called the "release node" is tied in the end of this cord and is held during the wind-up, but released upon firing.

A stone or some other projectile is placed in the socket for ammunition. The "hurler" then holds the ends of the two cords in his throwing hand and rotates the sling above his head or to his side. The stone is held in place while swinging by centrifugal force. At the correct moment, the hurler lets go of the release cord, and the projectile flies forward in a line tangent to the circle of the swing.

The power of a sling is most impressive. It is like a bullet being shot from a human gun. It will travel as far or farther than an arrow shot by a skilled archer. On impact, it can crush skulls, pierce an unprotected body, or smash out the windshield of a car. Accuracy comes with practice, and can be very precise.

11

We will look at some of the advantages of the sling as a weapon.

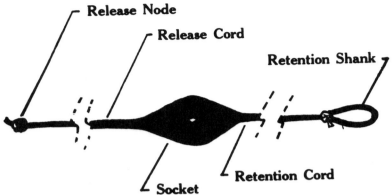

Illustration of a basic sling with parts named.

Advantages of the Sling as a Weapon

Ammunition

The basic ammunition used in a sling is stones or small rocks. Obviously, this kind of ammunition is abundant. There is very little effort involved in acquiring and storing it. Also, it free! You can't beat the cost of ammunition when it comes to the sling!

In the case of more sophisticated ammunition, such as ball bearings or lead sinkers, ammunition is still readily available at low prices. Ammunition can be stored without danger to children or pets. Its "shelf life" is unlimited, as the ammunition is not noticeably affected by moisture or extremes in temperature.

Silent

The sling is a very quiet weapon. The only sound it makes is a slight whir as you swing it. Yet it is deadly. This makes the sling a good weapon for hunting. It also means you don't have to worry about disturbing the neighbors when you practice (unless, of course, you put out one of their windows!).

Powerful

The sling is an extremely powerful hand-held weapon. In his article "The Sling as a Weapon," (see *Bibliography*) Manfred Korfmann estimates that a missile from a sling can achieve speeds of nearly 100 miles per hour! Such a missile can easily pierce an unprotected body (witness David against Goliath). The historian Vegetius said that sling missiles were deadlier than arrows against opponents clad in leather armor.

Accurate

With practice, one can become extremely accurate with a sling. After a day or two of practice, you should be able to hit a stump from at least 25 yards away. After a week of practice, you could hit a motionless bird from as much as 50 yards. Witness this testimony from a European traveler: "I have seen a native (of New Britain) knock a bird off a tree at about a hundred yards distance; they seldom pitch a stone further from the object aimed at than three or four yards." *(A Glossary of the Construction, Decoration and Use of Arms and Armor in All Countries and in All Times.)*

In the days of old, Balearian slingers would practice slinging stones through a narrows hoop at a distance of over 50 yards. In short, a practiced hurler could choose *which shoulder* of an opponent to hit from a minimum distance of fifty yards.

Easily Improvised

One of the nicest features of the sling is its simplicity. A sling can be constructed in a matter of seconds from any piece of cloth at least three feet long. Even in tight situations, possibilities for constructing a sling abound. You could tear a length of cloth out of your shirt or pants and have a crude, but functional, sling in seconds if the need arises.

Good Range

For a small weapon, the sling has a substantial range. Using stones, one can easily exceed 100 yards with practice. Specially designed missiles will double that distance. With practice, a good sling, and specially designed bullets, a crack slinger could hurl a missile 400 yards. *(The Poor Man's Armorer)*

An important factor in determining the potential range of a hurl is the length of a sling. A sling with two feet of cord on each end of the socket will cast a stone 50-75 yards. Three feet on each side will increase that to 75-100 yards. There is a limit on the size of sling you can comfortably use. Obviously, a ten foot length of cord wouldn't send a stone even six inches.

Highly Portable

The sling is so lightweight that it can be carried anywhere without discomfort. It does not have to be put in a special case; a pocket in your jacket would be more than enough room. It's hard to imagine a weapon deadlier than the sling weighing so little, and taking up so little room.

Easy To Conceal

Because of the sling's size and construction, it can be taken places where no other weapon can go. Unlike a bow and arrow or a rifle, it can be tucked inside of a pocket, easily out of sight. Since it is made of cloth, it will not trigger metal detectors like knives and guns will. A sling can easily be disguised to look like something else. It could be used as a handle on a suitcase, or a headband, or a piece of rope used to bundle a package.

Easy To Prepare For Use

Because the sling is portable and easy to conceal, it can be brought out from hiding and used instantaneously. There's no elaborate construction of all the pieces. There's no case to remove it from. You just pull it out and use it. If for some reason you had to break it down into two parts (the socket and two cords), they can be quickly reassembled for rapid use.

Multiple Uses

As we shall see, the sling can be used in a variety of ways other than as a weapon. Anything that you use a length of rope for, you can use a sling for. It substitutes excellently as a garrote, as a whip, as handcuffs or leg-ties. It can be used to safely fend off knife attacks, or a trip wire, or just to tie things together. It would be impossible to use most weapons in such a variety of situations.

Easy To Learn

It does not take years or even months to practice to acquire proficiency with a sling. After a few hours of practice, one could put the sling to valuable use. Within a week of practice, enough skill will have been acquired to use the sling successfully for hunting. You don't need a special field or arena to practice in, and there's no need to have others practice with you. It is hard to imagine someone taking lessons in the use of the sling. The motion is a natural one. With some simple instructions, you can become an expert slinger on your own.

Inexpensive

All in all, the sling is about as cheap a weapon as can be imagined. It can be constructed with ordinary materials found around the home. The ammunition most commonly used (stones) is found in abundance for free — no need to retrieve it after each shot. Places to practice are everywhere, and are also free. There is nothing like the sling when it comes to economical weaponry.

The Sling vs. The Bow

As an example of the differences between the sling and other weapons, we will compare this simple device to the bow and arrow. A bowman was often considered in the same class as a slinger in ancient warfare (see the History Chapter). This section will highlight both the advantages and disadvantages of the sling in practical situations.

Range
The sling is not limited by the device used to throw it as much as it is by the strength of the thrower. Because the aerodynamic qualities of a good stone are superior to those of an arrow, a good slinger can usually achieve greater range than a bowman.

A good bowman with a 60 lb. bow and a one ounce flight arrow might achieve a range of 300 yards. Ancient records show that good slingers using special one ounce aerodynamic sling "bullets" have attained ranges in excess of 400 yards (Iwasko, *Swinging the Sling*).

Effectiveness
When released with equal force, the sling bullet is much more powerful than an arrow due to the differences in their design. A good archer with a 60 pound bow can shoot an arrow that will travel about 150 feet per second with an energy of 25 foot pounds. A good slinger can hurl a one ounce lead missile at a speed of 190 feet per second with 36 foot pounds of energy (Iwasko). A sling bullet is much more dense than an arrow, and its force on impact is that much greater. Con-

sider the quote from a Spanish Conquistador in reference to Peruvian slingers:

> Their chief weapon... is the sling. With it they threw a large stone with such force that it could kill a horse. Its effect is indeed only slightly less than that of [a Spanish firearm]; I have seen how a stone flung from a sling over a distance of thirty paces broke in two a sword a man was holding in his hand. (Anonymous, *The Sling*, see *Bibliography*.)

Accuracy

It is in this area that the sling really has it over the bow! An arrow is subject to being diverted from its course by winds, but a sling bullet, once hurled, varies only slightly due to wind, precipitation, or other environmental factors. There are a great many written accounts which attest to the accuracy of the sling.

One historical example of the sling's accuracy comes from the Roman historian Livy, who states that the Acheans "would wound not merely the heads of their enemies, but any part of the face at which they might have aimed." (Korfmann)

Both the bow and the sling require practice to achieve accuracy, but for the time spent, one can become a deadly shot in no time with a sling compared to a bow. From my own studies, I have found that, using the "Overhand Hurl," you should at least be able to hit a tree trunk at 50 yards after a couple hours of practice. Not bad for a "primitive" weapon.

Other Advantages

There are a number of other qualities which make a sling preferable to a bow in many instances. First, a sling is highly portable and disguisable. It can be stuffed in any pocket. It can be secreted into buildings or any restricted areas without question. It can be brought out and prepared for use without attracting attention. The sling can also be transported without any special container or carrying case, and can fit into the glove compartment of an automobile. The sling is perhaps the ideal long-range weapon when concealment is of primary concern.

Because the sling is so small, its weight and size don't cause any hardship on its user. A powerful bow is usually fairly large, and it takes some skill just to maneuver it properly, much less to shoot it. Today's compound bows, though much more powerful weapons than a sling, are heavy and require a fair expenditure of energy just to hold them upright. Holding a compound bow can cause strain on the arms after only a few minutes. This is never the problem with a sling. Even when loaded, it is effortless to hold it and to position oneself for the shot.

Another main advantage of the sling over the bow is that it is so much more inexpensive. A good bow will cost you hundreds of dollars. Even the cheapest arrows are expensive and ones that provide any sort of accuracy are very costly, indeed. The initial investment for someone taking up the sport of archery will run a minimum of a hundred dollars.

On the other hand, the sling is nearly the cheapest weapon available beyond throwing rocks or using a club. A superb sling can be manufactured for about one dollar and an hour's time. Even the most deluxe type of sling would cost you less than ten dollars. The most common sort of ammunition is *free* — you just pick up a stone and sling it. And unlike arrows, you don't have to worry about retrieving your ammunition. Sophisticated ammunition for the sling (round steel ball bearings) can be bought cheaply by the hundreds, and only need to be used in important situations. Stones will do for practice.

Conclusion

You can see that the sling has many advantages over the bow. Depending on what your needs are, the sling could be the kind of weapon that a bow could never replace. Of course, modern compound bows are much more powerful and even more accurate than the sling. They are also much more expensive, much more difficult to conceal, and take a great deal more effort to master. Also, bows are considered lethal weapons in most places in the United States, and there are restrictions on their transportation and usage. While a sling may be covered by weapons statutes in some states, it is hard to imagine being arrested for the possession of one, and it would be next to impossible for anyone to discover that you possessed one unless they caught you in the act of shooting.

So why has archery become such a fine science while slinging is thought of as only an ancient, primitive skill? The main reason for the decline in sling usage was the introduction of plate armor in around 400 A.D. The sling could not easily penetrate such armor, whereas the pointed tip of the arrow could cut through. Also, archery has a sort of snob appeal today, whereas the only people who take pride in their ability to use a sling are predominantly ghetto youth. There is a chance that the sling may make a comeback as more and more restrictions are placed on the ownership and use of weapons. In urban street combat, there is not much that can match a sling, for the reasons mentioned above. On the streets, a cultured archer would be dead before his bow is drawn. Archery may be classy, but slinging is tough and practical!

4

Techniques of Use

In this chapter we will demonstrate how the sling is used. The techniques described and the illustrations provided should not only enable you to begin practicing the sling safely, but will help you to improve you technique and master new skills as you develop.

There is no substitute for practice; it will be impossible for you to learn to use the sling just from reading this book. However, you will see amazing results with only a minimum of time in the field, and before long you will have mastered a new and valuable defensive skill.

Throughout this chapter, we refer to the right hand as the throwing hand, the right leg as the throwing leg, etc. If you are left-handed, it will be an easy matter to just reverse the direction.

Preliminary Considerations

Safety

The safest place to use the sling is away from people and valuable property. Some people may not like your slinging, and there are laws that prohibit the use of the sling (a lethal weapon). Someone that wanted to make trouble for you could. You can avoid this by keeping out of their way, and making sure you aren't close enough to any valued property to damage it with a wild throw.

While having an audience may be fun, it is not a good idea when you are just starting to learn to sling. Try to stay away from crowded areas and well traveled public places. If you are on the beach, say, and some tourists come strolling along, just resist the temptation to show off, and give your arm a rest. Wait until they have passed a safe distance before continuing. Your stunning display of skills could turn a pleasant afternoon into a nightmare should you send someone to the emergency ward.

If you are slinging with two or more persons, make sure that everyone stays safely out of the way of the slinger. No matter how much confidence you have in your throw, you must remember that this is a DEADLY weapon. When a bad throw can be a matter of life or death, it is wise to place caution above confidence. In particular, make sure that no one stands behind the slinger when shooting, because that is the most common direction for wild shots to go. If the slinger is doing a helicopter hurl, then bystanders should sit or squat down during the throw, since the stone could fly in any direction, but usually at about eye level height.

Be sure to release the sling on the power stroke. This not only saves bystanders from injury, but also the slinger. If you don't let go at the right moment, the sling can easily get out of control. Many a good slinger has come home from a day of practice with large bruises or welts on the legs, and even on the head. Don't be in too big a hurry to master this new skill and you will return from your practice intact.

When using stones for ammunition, make sure they fit comfortably in the socket of the sling, and that they are rounded. Oversized and odd-shaped stones can easily fly out of the sling at odd moments or in wild directions. It's fun to experiment with irregularly shaped stones, but it's wise not to practice with them when you have other people around.

Lastly, keep your sling in top condition. It's smart to have two slings with you, so you won't be tempted to use a faulty sling that looks like it may still hold up. Of special concern are the places where the cords attach to the socket. This connection will hold up better if the cords are sewn into the socket, not tied. When you see them fraying or coming loose, stop slinging until they are repaired. Also watch the retention shank that fits around your finger, as this is another location where slings tend to break.

Location

The one thing required when practicing the sling is lots of open space. An ideal location, particularly if you are using rocks for ammunition, is the shore of a large body of water. There you will find abundant supplies of ammunition, and unobstructed space in which to hurl. Practicing by the water is also fun because floating logs make for good moving targets. Also, it's easy to gauge your distance by watching your stones splash down.

Other good locations are railroad tracks and open fields. You many find fewer stones in these places, and the rocks you do find will not be as rounded as beach stones. Still, you will not have obstructions to your hurling, and you should still have good vision of where your projectile lands.

City streets are definitely not a good place to practice with the sling. No matter how proficient you are with the sling, there is always the chance that a rock will slip or your sling will break. Rocks can easily fly off in unpredictable directions. Shattered windows and injured bystanders are two of the casualties that could result from using the sling in crowded urban places. It's wisest to get out of congested areas for practice.

Try to stay away from roadways when you are slinging. If you are in an open field or at the beach, this should be easy to do. If there is a roadway near where you practice, try to be sure that you are far enough from it that even a wild shot forcefully thrown could not reach a passing car or cyclist. Always have your back to the roadway, so that the intended direction of your shots is away from traffic.

Fundamentals

How It Works

The sling is childishly easy to operate. It consists of an oval (or "diamond-shape") patch of material called the socket, which holds the projectile. The socket is securely attached to a long cord on both sides, as shown in the diagram on the next page. The cord leading off the right is called the retention cord, and the cord to the left is the release cord.

23

At the end of the retention cord is a small loop called the retention shank, which is slipped over a finger on the throwing hand (we will describe exactly how to hold the sling below). At the end of the release cord is a knot called the release node. This node is also held in the throwing hand, as will be described later on.

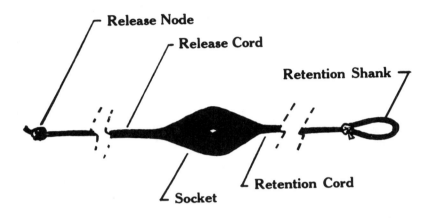

Illustration of a basic sling, with parts named.

When using a sling, a rounded stone is placed in the socket. Holding the ends of both cords in the throwing hand, the sling is rapidly rotated either to the side or over the head, or some combination of both. At the proper moment, the release node is dropped, and the stone hurls forward.

The sling works on the principle of centrifugal force. As you whirl the sling, the stone wants to "take off." The only think keeping it back is the socket. When the release node is dropped, the force of the stone pushes the socket inside, and the stone flies freely.

Generally speaking, the shorter the two cords of the sling, the less powerful the throw. The force of the throw is proportional to the radius of the swinging circle. A shorter cord can be released quicker than a long one, but the stone will have much less speed. An excessively long set of cords, on the other hand, would prove cumbersome and difficult to control and could be dangerous. A happy medium will allow for quick release of the stone, yet provide all the power and speed necessary without becoming too awkward to use quickly.

As you read these instructions and practice with your sling, you will develop the skills necessary to aim the stone, to build the greatest force behind it, and to design a sling suited to your ability and needs.

Holding The Sling

To be safe and to manipulate the sling properly, it is important that you understand how to hold it. Extend your throwing hand as shown below. Slip the retention shank over your middle finger. Some sources say that the sling operates better when the retention shank is placed over the ring finger. However, my own practice and use of the sling has led me to prefer the middle finger. Try them both for yourself, and do whatever feels right.

Next, hold the release node in the small space where your index and middle finger come together. There is a little room in there where the node should fit comfortably. Your thumb should come down on top of this knot so that the release cord is held between the thumb and index finger, as shown.

Now close your hand into a fist while maintaining your grip on the release node. The tip of your thumb should be just tucked inside of your curved index finger, so that it is still resting on top of the release node. The release cord and the retention cord should leave the top of your fist side-by-side. If you have the correct positioning, you are ready to proceed to the next step.

Stance

The fundamental point to remember when getting set to throw the sling is to RELAX. Don't worry about being a crack shot your first time out. You will find that the slinging motion is a very natural one, almost instinctive. If you are tense or jerky, you may release the sling too early or too late, with the result that the stone flies up instead of out. If there are bystanders (see section on safety), your tension could result in a serious accident. So relax — the rest will come easy.

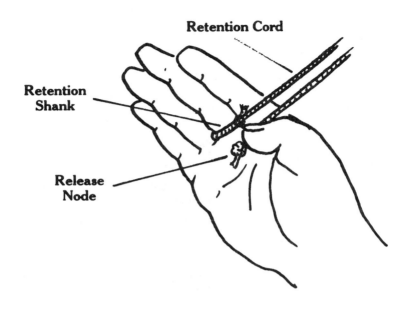

Retention Cord

**Retention
Shank**

**Release
Node**

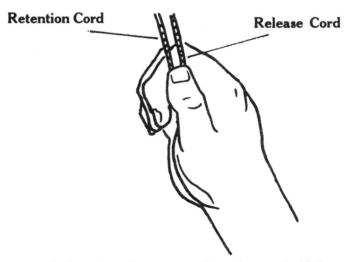

Retention Cord

Release Cord

How to hold the sling. Top picture shows how to hold the cords.
Bottom picture shows cord positioning before hurl.

First relax the arm and shoulder muscles. It doesn't take much practice time with the sling for your arm and should to get a little sore. To help you relax, and to prevent soreness, I recommend that you do a few stretching exercises immediately before slinging.

An illustration of a proper, relaxed slinging stance.

Now stand in a relaxed position facing your target. Your feet should be about shoulder distance apart with your left foot (non-throwing foot) one step ahead of your right foot. The toes of your left foot should point straight ahead while your right foot should point out to the side. See the illustration above for proper stance.

Once you are in the proper stance, you're ready to get loaded! Reach down and pick up a nice smooth stone that fits comfortably in the palm of your hand. If you grabbed a stone with irregular edges, or one that weighs a pound and a half, throw it back down and get another one. It should feel just right in your hand, and look like it will fit in the socket.

Holding the ends of the two cords in your throwing hand, place the stone in the socket and pull it *tightly*. Squeeze the stone into the socket so that it sits well. Imagine yourself as the powerful Greek peltist preparing to do in the enemy soldier. Now gently let the sling slip down so that it hangs down the right side of your body. Adjust the length of the release cord so that the two cords are the same length. Take in more of the release cord to shorten it, let out more cord to lengthen it. You are now ready to begin your first throw!

The Basic Hurl

The first time you go out slinging will be a humorous event. You will pick up a stone, slip it into the socket, start winding up, and the stone will fall out. In fact, the stone will fall out the first three or four times you begin to sling.

After a few tries, you will get the stone to stay put in the socket. Then you will wind up and throw, only to find yourself running for cover, wondering where the stone went. After a couple more throws, you will get the stone to fly in the desired direction (approximately). It will probably soar all of about 10 feet before thudding to the ground.

The process will continue for the first half hour, but don't get discouraged. After ten minutes, you will almost never have the problem of the stone falling out of the socket. In a half hour's time, you will no longer be making wild throws in unknown directions. Within an hour, you will be coming fairly close to a target fifty feet away. From then on, it's just a matter of refining your throw. You will be a slinger after just one day of practice; it will take a little more time to become an expert slinger.

The sling throw (called a "hurl") can be conveniently divided into two parts. The first part is the *wind-up*, where the sling gains momentum and the direction of the hurl is established. The second part is the *release*, where the stone is sent speeding toward its target. It's easy to think of a baseball pitcher doing a wind-up and then the delivery.

We'll look at each of these stages in turn. During the following discussion we will often refer to directions of a clock face. For example, the sling moves clockwise during an underhand wind-up, counterclockwise during an overhand wind-up. The sling is said to be at "six o'clock" when it's at its lowest point, and at "twelve o'clock" at its highest point. Try to visualize this metaphor of the rotating sling as the hand of a clock before you go on to read the following instructions.

The Wind-Up

When you are in the proper stance with the loaded sling to your side, begin to gently rock it back and forth. When you have a little momentum built up, start swinging the sling in a clockwise circle. This is the stage where the stone is mostly likely to slip free (which is a good thing, since it won't have had time to built up deadly momentum). If you stone slips, try a smaller, more rounded one, and *squeeze* it firmly into the socket before beginning again.

By the time you get the sling through one revolution there should be almost no chance of the stone slipping out. Continue to whirl the sling with the same motion. This is the whole extent of the wind-up. Once you have the sling revolving comfortably, you are ready to begin the release stroke. But there are some fine points of the wind-up which are particularly important for the beginner to understand. Let's take a look at them.

First, the wind-up is primarily a motion of the wrist, *not* the arm. You keep the sling in motion by an easy rotation of the wrist. You should not be using your whole arm as an extension of the sling; that is, your arm should not move in a clockwise fashion. It is only the sling that moves like the hands of a clock. There is a reason for the long cords of the sling: *they* do the swinging, while your arm provides the energy. For an example of the arm position during the wind-up, see the illustration of the underhand hurl, below.

For most hurls, the upper (from shoulder to elbow) is tucked tightly along your side. The upper arm barely moves during the wind-up. Your forearm (from elbow to wrist) extends out from the right side of your body to keep the sling from hitting you. The sling needs to be kept a safe distance from your side to swing freely. Most of the wind-up work is done with a gentle rotation of the wrist. The sling is designed so that the rotation is easy and natural — it shouldn't be forced or wild.

The second point to understand about the wind-up is that you don't have to whirl the sling a dozen times before releasing the stone. Long wind-ups are without a doubt the most common mistake made by beginning slingers. It seems like a longer wind-up would increase the force of the throw, but nothing could be further from the truth.

Once you start practicing slinging, you will see that the stone has no more momentum on the fifth rotation than it did on the fourth. The purpose of the wind-up is to steady the sling and bring it up to speed. This can be accomplished with as little as one rotation, and certainly no more than four. The customary wind-up is three rotations, but it can be accomplished with just one. Vegetius encouraged his slingers to release their missiles after only one swing so as to increase the rate of fire.

The real power of a hurl comes from the release stroke. The only thing a slinger accomplishes with long wind-ups is the rapid wearing out of his arm and shoulder. You would get very sore within an hour of practice, and yet have only taken a relatively small number of shots for the time spent. Such prolonged wind-ups would be similar to a baseball pitcher swinging his arm around six times before the pitch. No matter how good his arm, that pitcher would burn out before he ever hit the big time.

Now that you understand the wind-up, we'll examine the release stroke and see how it packs potency into a hurl.

The Release

Once you have gotten the sling balanced and up to speed with the wind-up, you are ready to let your stone fly. The release stroke is just like a wind-up stroke, only more powerful. You really put everything you've got into the last rotation, and drop the release cord at precisely the right moment. It will take some practice time before you can accurately hurl the proper distance in the correct direction. But you will see that improvement is fast to come — and fulfilling.

Your throwing arm and shoulder come more into play when you are ready to release the sling. On the final wind-up rotation, your upper arm moves backward and your shoulder rises up.

30

With your elbow sticking out behind you, whip the sling around its last arc and let it fly!

During the release stroke, your weight moves first from your left foot back onto your right foot. As you let the stone go, all of your weight then moves forward onto your front foot again. This shifting of weight is very similar to that of the baseball player as he delivers the pitch. When all your weight moves forward as you deliver your shot, your back foot will naturally lift off the ground slightly and move forward with your momentum (see the illustration of the overhand hurl). In this way, the maximum force is packed into your shot. Watch as the stone soars toward its target!

At the moment of release, the stone will continue its motion, traveling in a line tangent to the circle of rotation. For example, using the underhand throw, the wind-up will be clockwise. If the sling is released at six o'clock (the lowest point of rotation) it will travel straight forward. Released at nine o'clock, it will fly straight up. At twelve o'clock, the liberated stone will fly backwards.

An understanding of which direction the stone will fly is crucial to developing your aim. As we shall see when examining the different hurling styles, knowing the proper moment to release the sling is a tricky matter. Fortunately, this understanding comes easily with practice.

Let's recap what we've learned about the basic hurl. First, limber up and relax before you start practicing. Find a stone and get into the proper stance: left foot forward, right foot pointing out to the side. Load the sling and let it drop to your side. Start rotating the sling, using your wrist to do all the work. After a couple rotations, lean back, whip the sling around for the last time with a powerful jerk of the arm, then let the stone fly when the sling is in the right position.

Now that you know the fundamentals of slinging, we'll go on to look at the different types of throws you can use. Some of them are easy to learn, while others will require many hours of practice to master. All of them are fun!

Standard Hurls

Underhand Hurl

This is perhaps the easiest throw to learn. During this throw, the sling is swung clockwise to your right side (or throwing side). You begin in the hurling stance described above. Load your sling with a stone. Hold the socket and stone with your left hand out in front of you, and adjust the length of the cords until they are even. You are now ready to begin to hurl.

Drop the sling from your left hand so that it arcs down and swings backwards slightly. With a gentle snap of your wrist, bring the sling up again and start twirling it in a clockwise motion. This is the wind-up. Again, the motion is centered in your wrist, and most of your weight on your forward (left) foot.

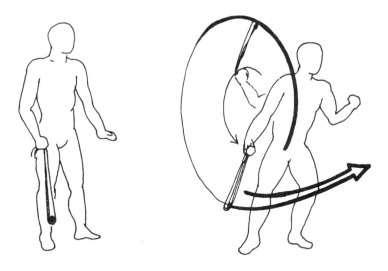

**The Underhand Hurl. The initial stance is shown on the left.
The wind-up is accentuated in the hurl on the right.**

After a couple of rotations, go into your release stroke. You should be looking straight ahead with your body pointed in the direction of your target. Just *after* the sling reaches its lowest point of the circle (approximately seven o'clock), let go of the release node. If all went well, the stone will arc slightly upward, fly into the distance, then descend toward the target.

Be sure to put the force of your body into the release. You will probably find that the first target you selected was much farther than your throw. Don't worry. As you become familiar with the motion and learn to time your release, you will soon be able to peg your target or surpass it if you choose.

Choosing the moment of release is the crucial factor determining the accuracy of your shot. A moment too soon, and the stone will slam into the earth in front of you. A moment too late and it will fly straight up into the heavens. A common mistake for beginners is to release the stone at nine o'clock, when it is straight in front of you. From this position, the stone will fly *up* — not *out*. Remember, the projectile continues in the direction it was traveling when released. At nine o'clock, that direction is up.

My own experiences and everything I have read about the sling has convinced me that the timing of the release comes naturally, even instinctively, with practice. Some people have a talent for it, others struggle to learn it. It is a difficult feeling to describe. When you know it's right, go with it. Your instincts will quickly align with your experience of how the stone flies, until after a while it becomes second nature.

Putting it all together, the underhand throw begins by loading the socket, letting the sling fall backward in an arc, then swinging the stone back up in a clockwise motion. After two or three full swings, put everything you've got into the final rotation, and let the stone fly just after it reaches its lowest point. Then watch it shoot toward your target!

Overhand Hurl

The overhand throw is the second basic throw. During this hurl, the sling is rotated counterclockwise to your right side (or throwing side). Begin in the basic hurling stance. Load your sling while holding it out in front of you, and adjust the cords so they are of even length. You are now ready to begin to hurl.

Like the underhand throw, you gently drop the sling so that it arcs down and backwards. Unlike the underhand hurl, you continue moving the sling in a counterclockwise direction, bringing it up behind you into a rotation. This is the wind-up. The motion is concentrated in your wrist as you whirl the sling counterclockwise.

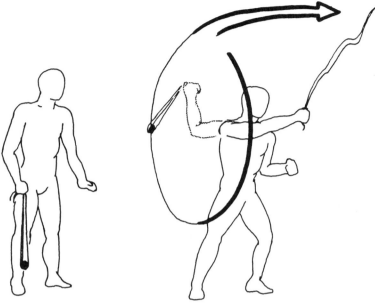

The Overhand Hurl. The initial stance is shown on the left, and the release stroke is shown on the right.

After a couple rotations, go into your release stroke. Concentrate your attention on your target. Just as the sling reaches the peak of its rotation (twelve o'clock), drop the release node. Like every other hurl, you must put your weight and strength into the release stroke if you want to get distance. Your weight goes forward to your non-throwing foot, and your arm really snaps that sling around as you let go.

There is a very little arc when the overhead throw is used. Since the stone starts out at a good height, it does not need to gain altitude to keep flying. Whereas the underhand throw is the "pop-up" of slinging, the overhand throw is the "line drive." The stone will move forward forcefully, descending only slightly as it moves toward the target.

Again, determining the exact moment for release is the key to accuracy. If you hesitate and let the sling pass twelve o'clock before release, it will crash into the earth. If you release it too soon, it will arc up then drop straight down. The proper moment for release is right at twelve o'clock, *no sooner or later*. If you want a little arc in your throw, release the stone just before it reaches its peak.

Helicopter Hurl

The helicopter hurl is a fun and fancy throw, but it is difficult to master. I recommend that you don't try this hurl until you are comfortable with the underhand and overhand shots. This is because the helicopter hurl is a very dangerous shot if the stone flies out early, as we shall see.

For the helicopter hurl, the sling is swung over the hurler's head like the top blades of a helicopter. You begin in the same stance as before, only this time you load the stone while holding the sling centered over your head. Because gravity will quickly pull the sling down, you must begin this throw with a firm wind-up. Holding the sling as shown in the picture below, begin whirling it above your head in a *clockwise* motion.

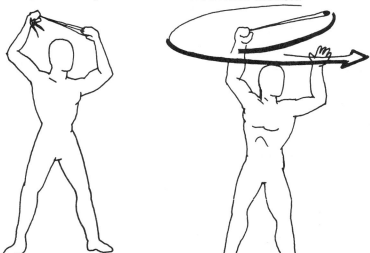

The Helicopter Hurl. Initial stance is shown on the left, while the release stroke is illustrated at right.

Just as the arm does not come into play until the release stroke with the other hurls, so too with the helicopter. The upper arm from shoulder to elbow should project out to the right of your body on a line with your shoulder (as shown). The forearm is extended straight up into the air on the right side of your head. This keeps the sling rotating safely above your head during the wind-up. The wind-up motion is performed by the wrist, as in the other throws.

During the release stroke, the forearm comes into play. On the final rotation, swing with the whole forearm to pack force into your throw. Your body weight will again go forward onto your non-throwing foot. To hurl the stone in the direction your body is pointed, release the node when the sling is farthest to the right of your body. The stone will fly forward with very little arc.

The beauty of the helicopter hurl is that it allows you to aim the stone in any direction without moving your whole body. With the underhand and overhand throws, you must physically face your target for an accurate throw. Not so with the helicopter. If you release the stone at the right-most point of rotation, it will fly in the direction your body is pointed. If you release it in front of you, it will fly to your left; if you release it to you left, it will fly behind you; if you release it behind you, it will fly to the right.

This feature means that, from one position, the stone can be hurled in any compass direction. This makes the helicopter hurl an ideal throw to use when hunting; if your prey is on the move, you can quickly and easily alter the direction of your throw. The only directions you can't hurl in from this position are straight up or straight down, neither of which are usually desired.

Because of its multi-directional capabilities, the helicopter hurl is a particularly dangerous throw. With the underhand and over-hand hurls, a wild stone will most likely travel straight up or straight down — at the worst, it will fly backwards. But with the helicopter hurl, a wild shot will travel at a deadly height in any conceivable direction *except* up or down. Don't learn this shot when spectators are around. Only demonstrate it once you have mastered the basic technique.

Comments On The Standard Hurl

These three throws, the underhand, the overhand, and the helicopter, are the major three hurls used in slinging. Each has its advantages and disadvantages, which we will discuss. Also, human beings are made differently; some will find the helicopter throw less comfortable than the underhand throw, others will find the opposite to be true. You will probably come to prefer one style over the others, and make that your standard throw.

The Underhand Throw. This throw is probably the easiest one to learn. The motion is comfortable and familiar. The advantage of this throw is that it is very accurate at long distances. It seems that one can put more force into the underhand throw than the overhand throw, because of the ease of swinging the arm in the clockwise direction.

The disadvantage of the underhand throw is that it involves more arc than is often desirable, rather than flying in a straight line. For baseball fans, the underhand throw is more like a fly ball than a line drive.

The reason for all the arc is that the stone is released at its lowest point. If the stone were released exactly at six o'clock, it would fly too close to the ground and probably land early. In order to get both distance and height, the stone is released shortly after its lowest point, so that it arcs up then down toward its target.

You'll have to get used to the arc of the underhand throw. You can adjust the arc to your needs. The later the release, the greater the height of the arc. The earlier the release, the less the arc, and the lower the stone will fly. Experiment with the timing of your release so that you can master the flight path of your stone and aim with accuracy.

The Overhand Throw. This throw is more difficult to learn and control than the underhand throw. That's because the human arm seems less willing to revolve in a counterclockwise direction than in a clockwise direction. This throw is well suited to short-range targets, because it will not have much force, but will have a straight flight pattern.

The flight pattern is the big advantage of this throw. Since the sling is released at its uppermost point, it doesn't fly too close to the ground. Consequently, there is very little arc in this throw. Ideally, the stone will descend steadily on a straight line once it is discharged. This throw is like the overhead baseball pitch, or a line drive.

Again, you can modify your timing when releasing the stone to get the desired results. Releasing the sling slightly after its peak point will cause it to descend sharply and rapidly. Such a throw would be ideally suited to hitting a very close target with a great deal of force. Releasing the stone at its peak will cause it to descend more gradually. Such a release would be perfect for hitting a target within about 25 yards.

If you experiment with the timing of your release, you will soon learn exactly how to get the throw you want. It is the timing of the release more than anything else that determines the accuracy of the throw. An expert slinger will be able to control the exact moment of release. This takes time to learn, but is well worth the effort. The more you practice, the closer you will come to your target.

The Helicopter Hurl. This is the most difficult of the basic throws to learn. That is because it takes practice to balance the sling correctly during the wind-up. Poor balance will result in the circle of motion drooping about your head, so that the socket whizzes past your ear. The trick to proper balance is in the wrist. If your wrist is limber and rotates freely, you will have no problem with this throw.

This throw is excellent for long-range shooting on a straight line, with little or no arc. Unlike the underhand throw, the projectile discharges straight out from the sling, gradually descending toward its target. Also, the helicopter hurl does not descend as rapidly as the overhand throw.

Alternate between these throws as you practice, so that you become proficient at the many ways possible for handling a sling, and so your arm doesn't get worn out from repeating the same exact motion over and over again. It is good to practice with all the styles so that you can design a throw to your particular circumstances.

Combination Hurls

Once you have control over the three basic throws, you can start to build your own style. There are many possibilities for customizing your technique. Be careful, though, because this is the stage where ambitious slingers limp home from practice with large welts, bruises and other painful blemishes. Be certain to take the necessary safety procedures when learning these hurls.

The Figure Eight

This obscure but fancy throw is sure to wow the fans in the gallery. It is really a combination of the underhand and overhand throws. Load your sling, let it arc downward, and start into a clockwise rotation.

Once you have the sling in a balanced rotation, switch to a counterclockwise rotation. This is a very tricky maneuver. It requires use of the forearm as well as the wrist to maintain this rotation. The socket moves in a figure eight pattern, alternating from underhand to overhand wind-ups. The stone is usually released at the height of the counterclockwise rotation, though it can also be released at the lowest point of the clockwise rotation.

The figure eight is probably *the* most difficult hurl to master. The transition from underhand to overhand, and back, is very tricky. It's easy for the sling to lose momentum or get out of control. Just keep practicing, and you'll get it — but don't practice this throw with spectators around.

The nice advantage to the figure eight is that, once you get it going, it's a more balanced throw than the others. The sling tends to stay in one place instead of always moving out to the side, which can happen with the underhand and overhand throws. This quality of the figure eight make it easier to aim the stone the with other throws.

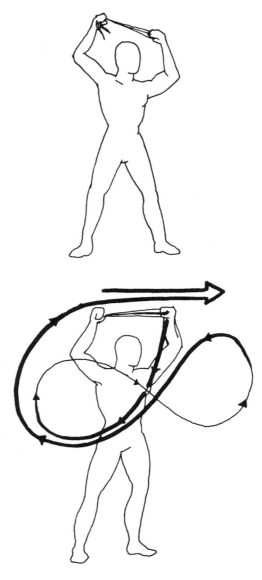

**The Figure Eight. Initial stance is shown on top,
while the hurl follows the pattern shown on the bottom.**

The Sidearm Sling

This throw is a combination of the helicopter hurl and the underhand hurl. You start in the helicopter position, and do the normal wind-up for that hurl. When you are ready for the release stroke, bring the sling down to about halfway between the helicopter position and the underhand position. Release the stone right as you achieve this midway position.

The release, being neither overhead nor underhand, is like a sidearm pitch in baseball. It makes for a more powerful throw than the helicopter or the overhand, yet doesn't have all the arc of the underhand hurl. I wouldn't be surprised if this becomes one of your favorite throws!

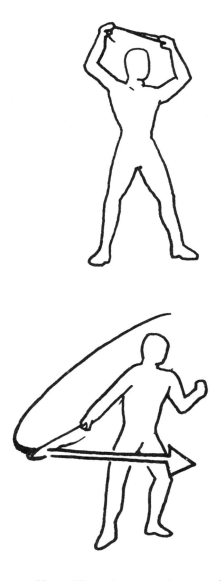

The Sidearm Sling. The release stroke goes from overhead to underhand in a quick, sidearm movement.

The Lariat

This throw takes its name from the cowboy rodeo. It is basically a figure eight with one little twist. With the figure eight, the sling moves through the "8" shape on the throwing side of your body, going from underhand to overhand and back again. With the lariat, you do the overhand rotation on the throwing side of the body, then an underhand rotation on the non-throwing side.

The motion is exactly like that of the cowboy in old westerns: you swing the sling from your right side to your left side, back and forth, repeatedly. You can either release the stone at the peak of the overhand rotation on your right side, or at the peak of the underhand rotation on your left side. The latter release is sort of a backhand flip — unique in all of slinging!

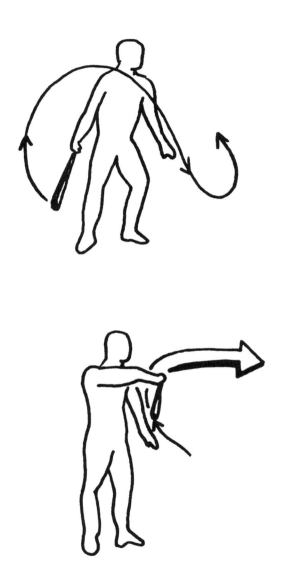

**The Lariat. The sling is flipped from one side of the body
to the other (top). It can be released underhand,
or with the unique backhand movement shown (bottom).**

44

5

Construction of The Sling

There are limitless possibilities for designing a sling to meet your needs. One of the nicest aspects of this weapon is that it is very simple to construct at home with readily available materials. A sling can be improvised from a stocking in seconds, or one could create an elaborate sling designed for the greatest possible range. In this chapter, we will show you how to construct a variety of slings, from the simple to the elaborate.

Materials And Sources

The basic material for a sling is a long piece of cloth. For emergency needs, this could be a piece of pillowcase, a sheet, a man's shirt, an automobile seat cover, or just about any available fabric. The most common material used to construct a sling is leather. It is also the preferred material (with some exceptions).

As you know by now, the basic design of the sling involves two cords attached to each side of a patch of material. The cords may vary in length from one foot to three and half feet long. They are usually narrow, though substantially thicker than string. We'll take a look at some materials and discuss their advantages and disadvantages.

Strips of leather are excellent material for cords. A good source of this material is leather boot laces. These may be a little thin for your purposes. Thicker leather cords can be cut from a patch of leather bought at a fabric store or taken from an old piece of clothing.

With high-tech in full gear, there are now a variety of sturdy materials to choose from at the local hardware store. Nylon cord is very strong, and holds up well under rigorous slinging conditions. It is a bit more slippery than leather when held, but it is also cheaper.

The socket can be made from any thick piece of cloth. Old clothing can be used for this, particularly if it is leather. A very common material used for the socket is the tongue of an old leather boot. The curvature is already there, and the material requires little cutting to achieve the correct size. You can probably get an old shoe tongue from a local cobbler or shoe repair store (for free).

There are some new materials on the market these days which make excellent slings. I have seen plastic screen material used for the socket. Although I don't know where you can get such plastic netting, I do know that it helps keep the wind resistance down. It also seems to hold up very well. Try your local hardware store or fabric store, and see if they know where you can get it. Ask them for "coated nylon scrim."

If you want to construct your own sling at home, the following tools will come in handy: a sharp knife capable of cutting through leather; a large sewing needle and sturdy thread; an awl, ice pick, or some other sharp instrument for poking holes; some string or twine; an egg-shaped rock. You will see below how all of these come into play. If you aren't the best at sewing, you might try to find someone to help you.

Design and Assembly

Basically, follow the pattern on the next page. If you have experience with the sling, you will want to adjust the length of the cords and the size of the socket to fit your style. The longer the cords, the greater the distance that can be achieved. However, if the cords are too long to be comfortably managed, it will decrease your range and will be dangerous to you and bystanders.

Ideally, the socket should be big enough to comfortably fit the size stone you are most likely to throw. Historical records show that the most frequently used stone was the size of a hen's egg,

46

and about the same shape, weighing approximately one ounce. The sling shown here is designed for such a stone. If you like to throw bigger or smaller stones, adjust the size of the socket so you won't have problems with the stone slipping out.

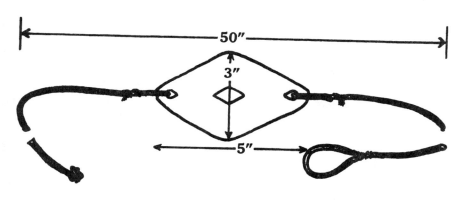

Plans for making a basic sling.

There are two ways to attach the cords to the socket. The first way is to cut slits into the ends of the socket, and tie the leather cords into them. Be sure to leave enough material between these slits and the edges of the socket so that the cords will not tear out. Use a slip knot or three half-hitches to tie the cords in securely.

The problem with this method is that the knots can loosen, and thus become dangerous. Also, the knots don't always want to stay in the proper place — they could move around enough to make it difficult to throw the sling the way it was intended to be thrown.

A superior method for attaching the cords is to sew them into the socket. Ideally, the cords should come from one long strip of leather. Cut a slit into the center of the strip long enough that each side of the slit can be sewn to the outside rim of the socket.

Then fold the socket over the slits in the cord, and sew the cord and socket together. This will create a durable sling that should provide many years of enjoyable sport.

Make the retention shank on the right-hand cord by tying a small loop in it using a bowline knot. The release node can be small or large. A small one requires only a single knot or two. A large release node can be made by simply increasing the number of knots tied in it. Be sure that you have accounted for the number of knots before determining the length of the cords, or they will be uneven.

The socket can be diamond shaped or oval. I prefer the oval, since it seems to fit the shape of the stone better. It is simple to cut a diamond shape, since it involves only straight cuts. The oval shape must be cut more or less freehand, though you can use a jar top as a guide when you are cutting.

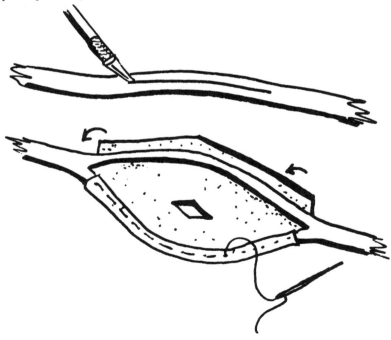

The best method for making a sling is to sew the cords into the socket. Cut a slit in the cord (top), then wrap the socket around the cords and sew them together (bottom).

When you cut the socket out of the material you are using, be sure to cut out enough extra material around the edges to sew the cords in. Then cut a circle or diamond shape hole in the very center of the socket. This hold helps the stone sit tightly during your wind-up, and also reduces air resistance. It should be about the size of a dime.

Once you have the socket cut out, use your awl or ice pick to punch holes into it. These holes are very helpful at reducing the air resistance you'll encounter when slinging. About a dozen or so of these holes should be adequate.

You now want to get the socket to adopt the proper curvature. When you have the sling finished and all assembled, take an egg-shaped stone and press it into the socket. Then fold the socket around the stone as far as possible. Then tie the stone into this position with the string or twine I suggested you have ready above. After you have tied up the stone, soak the whole thing in water and let it dry before untying the string. This will cause the leather to dry out around the stone, thus taking on the curvature of the stone.

The sling is given its final preparation by soaking it in water and letting it dry into the proper curvature.

You can also get the proper curvature in your socket just by using it. Every time you throw a stone, you firmly press it into the socket, and pull tightly on the two cords to force the socket to take the shape of the stone. But it is quicker and simpler to soak the socket with a stone in it ahead of time. I've found that an unfit socket is very frustrating when slinging — a lot more stones find their way free before they're supposed to.

Variations

You've just seen the basic style for the sling. Some variations and adaptations will be mentioned here.

In a pinch, a piece of old clothing will make a good temporary sling. The best method for using such materials is to make a one-piece sling (you can do this with leather, too). Cut or tear the material so that it is one long strip that widens out in the middle to about four inches, and narrows down to a half inch at the ends.

These kinds of slings are great in an emergency, but don't hold up to much use. A one-piece sling made out of leather, however, is even better than a sling with sewn-in cords. It will stand up to a lot of punishment, without any worry about the cords fraying where they join the socket. The only tricky part is finding a piece of leather that long. It may be worth the expense.

You can also use a piece of an old automobile tire for the socket, since it comes ready-made with the right curvature, or an old inner tube. Surgical tubing can be used for the cords to increase range. The increase in range, however, comes at the expense of controllability and accuracy. Also, the tubing will wear out faster than leather. Occasionally, you will find natural slings. A surgeon's mask is one good example. A bandanna, an Ace bandage, a necktie, and a soft belt are some other examples.

You can use fishing line or surgical thread for a cord that will have very little wind resistance. If you use these materials, though, the retention loop will cut into your finger. To avoid this problem, tie the cords to a metal ring wide enough to fit over your finger, and use the ring for the retention loop.

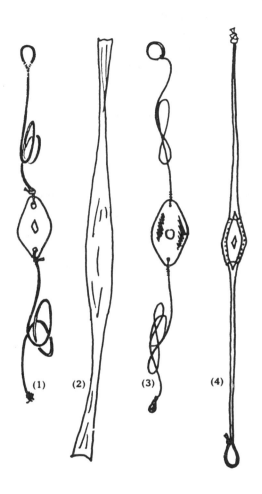

1) Standard sling with tied cords. 2) One-piece sling.
3) Sling with inner-tube socket, fishing line cords, and metal
retention right. 4) Standard sling with sewn-in cords.

51

The Staff Sling

One popular adaptation derived from the sling is a staff sling. The staff sling uses a stick or pole with a small sling socket attached to the top. It was widely used in the middle ages for hurling larger stones, weighing one pound or more. The staff sling is good for throwing greater weight, though it doesn't have the range or accuracy of the regular sling.

The length of the pole can vary from one foot to four feet or even more. The shorter staffs are swung sidearm, and make for a fairly powerful throw. The longer staffs are lowered behind the head, then swung over the head with the full force of the body. The longer staffs were used with the heaviest of stones.

The sling consists of a large socket and two short cords. One cord is tied anywhere from six inches to one foot below the top of the pole. The other cord is tied loosely around the end of the pole or knotted and slipped into a notch in the top of the pole. This second cord flies off as the staff is swung from either side or behind the head. The stone is thus free to fly towards its target. Two examples of the staff sling are shown on the next page.

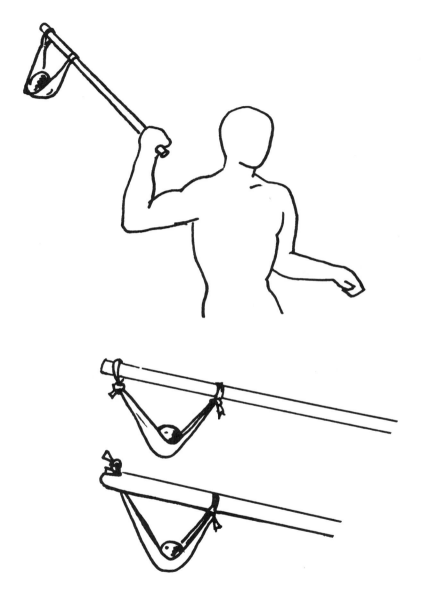

The staff sling in use (top). Two types of staff sling, the upper one with a loose loop to hold on socket, while the lower one uses a knot-and-notch system.

6

Ammunition

One of the joys of slinging as a sport is that the ammunition is cheap and readily available. The sling really has it over other weapons in this department. The abundance of sling ammunition makes it an ideal sport for someone on a limited budget. It also makes things easy on beginners, who don't have to go out and buy all sorts of fancy equipment.

Prehistoric man began slinging using stones as ammunition. As the sling grew more popular, smooth, rounded stones became fairly valuable. Archaeological digs have turned up storehouses of not hundreds, but thousands of these stones. The advantage of having uniform ammunition is that it allows slingers to improve their skill through consistency. In fact, if you really want accuracy in your shots, you'll have to use uniform stones.

About 5000 B.C., people started to manufacture sling bullets. The first ones manufactured were spherical. Later, the shape was changed to biconical (pointed at the end). The most popular design for sling missiles came to be the ovoid (like a hen's egg — pointed at one end and rounded at the other. (Korfmann)

The first manufactured missiles (about 7,000 years old) were made out of clay. The pure clay missiles were sun dried so they wouldn't crack. By classical Greek times, missiles were being made from lead. Archaeologists have found not only missiles from this period, but also the molds used to make dozens of pellets at a time.

Unlike a slingshot, which is limited in size and the shape of ammunition, the sling can hurl anything from pennies to bricks. The only restrictions on the type of ammo you use are: 1) that it will fit into the socket; and, 2) that you have the strength to hurl it.

Rocks are probably the most common ammunition used in the sling. They are not only plentiful, but *free* — no worry about retrieving your ammo for future uses! Certainly this is the type of ammunition you will want to use when starting out. As you develop your skills, however, you might want to see what can be done with more elaborate kinds of projectiles.

I have achieved the best results when slinging using rounded rocks that are about the size of a golf ball. Smaller stones work very well, too, but I like the resistance provided by the larger ones. It is hard to find ample supplies of stones larger than a golf ball that are smoothly rounded. If you go too big, you may find the strain on your arm excessive. I imagine someone hurling a large brick might find their arm traveling with the sling upon release.

For ideal results, the rocks should be as round as possible. It is fun to practice with a variety of shapes, though, just to see how they move. Flat objects will sometimes fly in bizarre patterns, seemingly defying gravity. After you have developed your skills, you can sometimes use flat stones to skip across the water. Skipping is great fun, both for the hurler and the audience!

For those who desire the accuracy of sophisticated ammunition, the best results can be achieved using steel ball bearings or lead sinkers. These deadly pellets can more than double your range. They are readily available from hardware stores, automotive parts outlets, or fishing supply stores (for lead sinkers). The best size is about one inch in diameter — but try out a variety and see what you like best.

If you are using the sling in a street/survival situation, you will find that there are few limits on the types of improvised ammo you can use. Aside from rocks and metal pellets, you can use fire darts, glass bottles, explosive devices, incendiary devices (molotov cocktails), customized objects (like a superball with protruding razor blades), or other imaginative missiles.

The advantages of a sling over hand throwing these devices is the increased power and range it affords. If you are a practiced

56

slinger, you will also find it more accurate than hurling with your hand. Of course, you should exercise extreme caution when using these deadlier forms of ammunition.

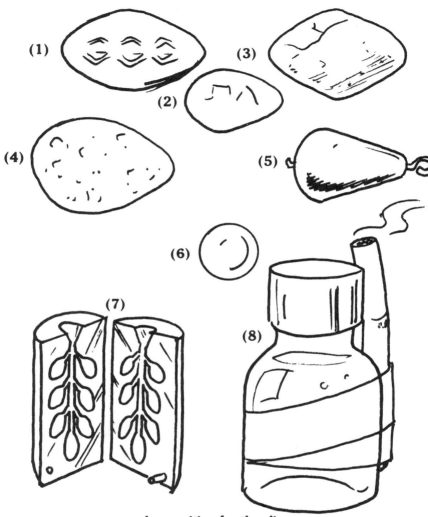

Ammunition for the sling.
1) Large molded lead missile.
2) Small molded lead missile.
3) Biconical clay missile.
4) Ovoid projectile chipped from stone.
5) Lead fishing sinker.
6) Steel ball bearing.
7) Ancient "tree" mold for manufacturing sling bullets.
8) Molotov cocktail.

Practical Applications

The sling is an incredibly versatile tool. It can be used in a great variety of situations, and there are some circumstances where any other weapon would be second best. The sling can provide entertainment and exercise, as with any other sport. It is also an important survival weapon. We'll look at some of its applications here. I'm sure you'll think of some others we haven't included.

Entertainment

Slinging stones is a great way to spend an afternoon in the out-of-doors. At the beach you can practice your technique while soaking up the rays. You'll have a great time skipping stones or pegging floating logs. Hurling will also help take the edge off a nasty day by providing an enjoyable and (hopefully) harmless way of releasing frustration or anger. It's also nice for those who enjoy quiet contemplation, tossing a stone every now and then for something to do.

Sport

Slinging is not recognized as a world-class sport, but that doesn't mean it's not suited to it. You can compete with friends for distance and accuracy. You can also adapt games to the sling. Sling golfing, where you sling a golf ball toward the pin rather striking it with a mallet, is one interesting application. You can also try slinging into hoops as a test of accuracy. Who knows, *sling bowling* could very well become the next outdoor sport craze!

Hunting

If you enjoy hunting, and want something a little more challenging than blowing away squirrels with a shotgun, the sling will put some variety in your chase. Nearly as deadly as a bullet, the sling is also supremely quiet. In the *Complete Book of Outdoor Lore*, Clyde Ormond says the sling "has ample power for knocking down small game and grouse at several rods." Try it — your family will be impressed with the rugged way you brought home dinner!

Agriculture

The sling has been a very useful tool in agriculture for centuries. David had acquired skill with the sling as a shepherd before he went against Goliath in the famous battle. Around the world, the sling has been used to keep predators away from flocks or herds of animals. The sling has also seen use keeping animals, like birds away from crops. In some places, the sling is even used to knock fruit out of trees!

Wilderness Survival

The sling is a must for campers, hikers, cross-country skiers, and others who enjoy the remote outdoors. Because it is light, the sling adds almost no weight to a backpack. Ammunition is abundant in the wilderness, and need not be carried along. In national forests and parks, where most weapons are prohibited, a sling can be taken in without arousing any attention.

The sling is an essential outdoor survival weapon because it acts as an insurance policy in case you get lost or injured. Small animals can be fairly easily dispatched with a sling — especially water fowl, where there are few obstructions to a clear shot. You will be amazed how accurate you can become when your life may depend on how well you shoot.

I never go into the woods without a sling. I may never use it for anything but entertainment, but I sure feel more comfortable knowing it's there if I need it.

Urban Warfare

The sling is increasingly becoming a preferred weapon for urban survival and warfare. With more and more weapons being banned or restricted, it is important to know how to use commonly available materials to defend yourself. An improvised sling can be manufactured in a matter of seconds (tear off a piece of sheet, knot it twice in the middle, and you have a deadly weapon). It is no surprise that slings are used regularly in street warfare in Northern Ireland.

The sling is a perfect urban survival weapon for many reasons. First, it is lightweight and compact for easy concealment. Second, it can be retrieved and prepared for use in no time at all. Third, it has a range that can be equaled only by a gun (it is hard to imagine someone using a bow and arrow as an urban survival weapon). Because of this range and power, it is far superior to a knife when there is some distance between the combatants.

The range of the sling allows it to penetrate the windows of very tall buildings. It is also quick enough to allow hitting a rapidly moving target; for example, it could be used to smash the windshield of an oncoming car. It can also be used to hurl objects which can't be held in the hand, like flaming missiles or projectiles with sharp edges.

The sling can even be improvised to use in close range combat. It can be used in the same way a belt is used to block the thrusts of an attacker with a knife. A sling with a firm leather socket could be wrapped around the fist to protect the hand and improve the results of blows in hand-to-hand combat. It can also be used to tie the hands or legs of a subdued opponent.

In short, there are many urban warfare situations where there is no substitute for the sling. For city dwellers on a low budget, there is nothing quite like the sling. Even if you own several kinds of weapons, your artillery is not complete without a sling. The sling is an inexpensive, easily-manufactured weapon that could just save your life.

8

Bibliography

Anonymous, *The Sling*. Ambassador Enterprises, Alliance, OH, undated, out of print.

Barrow, Bonnie & Clyde (editors), *The Poor Man's Armorer*, Volume One. Eureka, CA, 1978.

Blackmore, Howard L., *Hunting Weapons*. Walker & Company, NY, 1971.

Braidwood, Robert J., *Prehistoric Men*, 7th Edition. William Morrow and Company, NY, 1967,

Diagram Group, The, *Weapons*, St. Martin's Press, NY, 1980.

Encyclopedia Britannica. Articles on "Ammunition," "Sling," and "Weapons."

Hebden, Major E.N., *Weird and Wonderful Weaponry*. Enterprise Books, Secaucus, NJ, 1975.

Hogg, Brigadier O.F.G., *Clubs to Cannon*. Gerald Duckworth & Co., Ltd., London, 1968.

Holy Bible, The, King James Version. Books of "Samuel," "Judges," "2 Chronicles," and "2 Kings."

Iwasko, F. R., "Swinging the Sling." *Fur-Fish-Game*, May 1976.

Korfmann, Manfred, "The Sling as a Weapon." *Scientific American*, October 1973.

Norman, A.V.B. and Don Pottinger, *Warrior to Soldier, 499 to 1660*. Weidenfeld & Nicholson, Ltd., London, 1966.

Ormond, Clyde, *Complete Book of Outdoor Lore*. Harper and Row, NY, 1969.

Reid, William, *Arms Through the Ages*. Harper and Row, NY, 1976.

Saxon, Kurt (editor), *The Survivor*, Volume 3. Atlan Formularies, Harrison, AR, 1977.

Saxtorph, Niels M., *Warriors and Weapons, 3000 B.C. to A.D. 1700*. Blandford Press, London, 1972.

Sietsema, Robert, *Weapons & Armor*. Hart Publishing Company, Inc., NY, 1978.

Snodgrass, A.M. , *Arms and Armour of the Greeks*. The Camelot Press, Ltd., London, 1967.

Stone, George Cameron, *A Glossary of the Construction, Decoration and Use of Arms and Armor in All Countries and in All Times*. Jack Brussel, NY, 1961.

Tunis, Edwin, *Weapons — A Pictorial History*. World Publishing, NY, 1972.

Williams, Gene B., "When You Don't Have Weapons," *Survival Guide*, April 1982.

World Book Encyclopedia. Article on "Sling."

YOU WILL ALSO WANT TO READ: